THE ULTIMATE ANIMAL LIBRARY

Giraffes

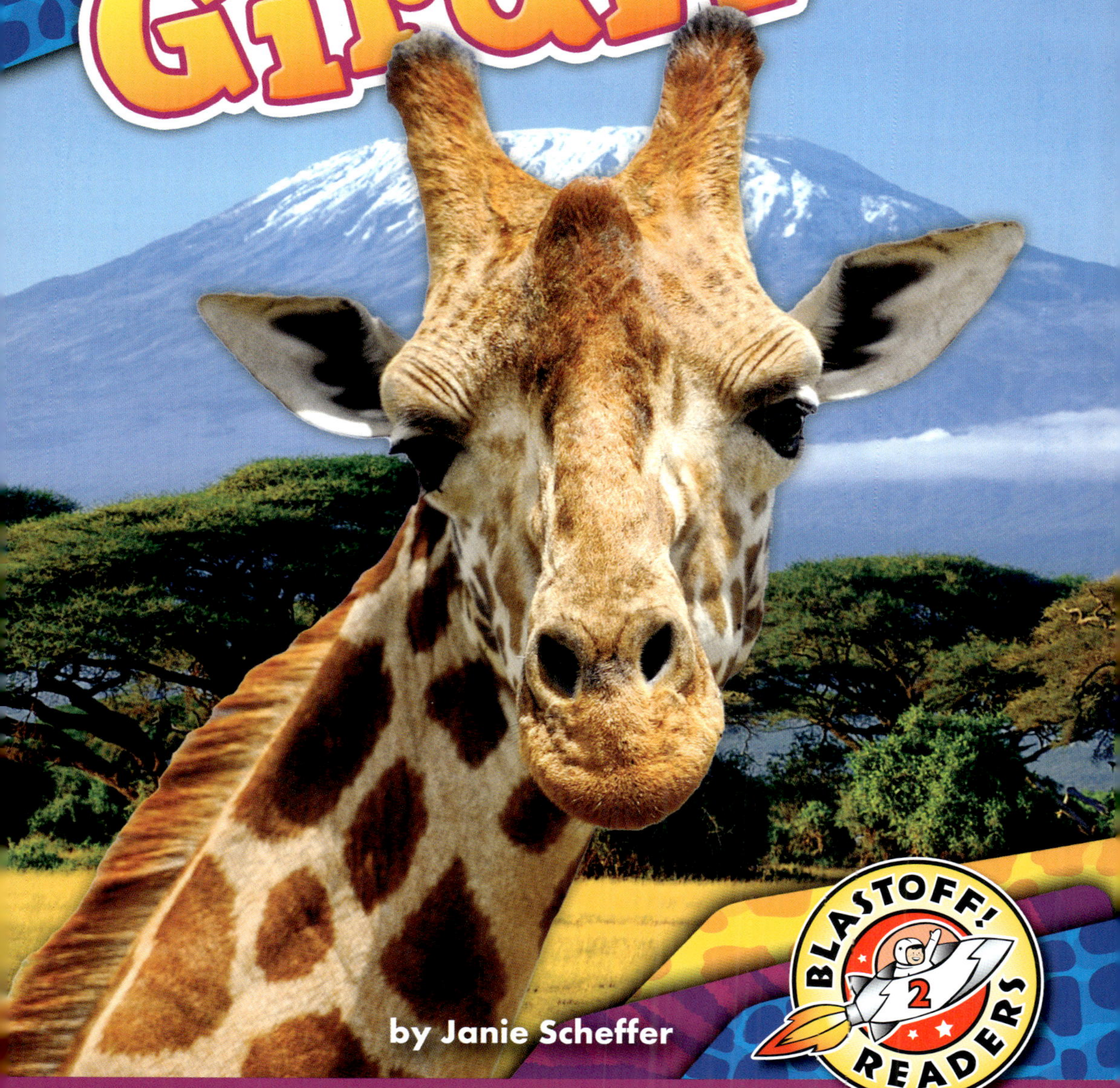

by Janie Scheffer

BLASTOFF! READERS 2

BELLWETHER MEDIA • MINNEAPOLIS, MN

Blastoff! Readers are carefully developed by literacy experts to build reading stamina and move students toward fluency by combining standards-based content with developmentally appropriate text.

Level 1 provides the most support through repetition of high-frequency words, light text, predictable sentence patterns, and strong visual support.

Level 2 offers early readers a bit more challenge through varied sentences, increased text load, and text-supportive special features.

Level 3 advances early-fluent readers toward fluency through increased text load, less reliance on photos, advancing concepts, longer sentences, and more complex special features.

★ **Blastoff! Universe**

Reading Level

Blastoff! Beginners — Grade K

Blastoff! Readers — Grades 1–3

Blastoff! Discovery — Grade 4

This edition first published in 2025 by Bellwether Media, Inc.

Library of Congress Cataloging-in-Publication Data

Names: Scheffer, Janie, 1992- author
Title: Giraffes / by Janie Scheffer.
Description: Minneapolis, MN : Bellwether Media, Inc., 2025. | Series: Blastoff! Readers: The Ultimate Animal Library | Includes bibliographical references and index. | Audience term: Juvenile | Audience: Ages 5-8 Bellwether Media | Audience: Grades 2-3 Bellwether Media | Summary: Relevant images match informative text in this introduction to giraffes. Intended for students in kindergarten through third grade"- Provided by publisher.
Identifiers: LCCN 2024038366 (print) | LCCN 2024038367 (ebook) | ISBN 9798893042382 library binding | ISBN 9798893043358 ebook
Subjects: LCSH: Giraffe--Juvenile literature
Classification: LCC QL737.U56 S344 2025 (print) | LCC QL737.U56 (ebook) | DDC 599.638--dc23/eng/20240927
LC record available at https://lccn.loc.gov/2024038366
LC ebook record available at https://lccn.loc.gov/2024038367

Editor: Elizabeth Neuenfeldt Series Designer: Veah Demmin

Printed in the United States of America, North Mankato, MN.

Table of Contents

What Are Giraffes?	4
Towers!	12
Growing Up	18
Glossary	22
To Learn More	23
Index	24

What Are Giraffes?

Giraffes are the tallest **mammals** on land. Their necks alone are 6 feet (1.8 meters) long! They live in many parts of Africa.

Giraffe Report

Range

Status in the Wild

Habitats

All giraffes have fur **coats**. Their coats can be light tan to dark brown.

No two giraffes look alike! Each giraffe has a different coat **pattern**.

Male giraffes can be 18 feet (5.5 meters) tall. Some weigh up to 4,255 pounds (1,930 kilograms).

Females are smaller than males.

Giraffes have at least two horns on top of their heads. They are called **ossicones**.

Giraffes have long legs. They can quickly run away from **predators**.

Spot a Giraffe

Towers!

Giraffes stand tall in forests and **savannas**.

They stay safe in groups called **towers**. Around 20 giraffes live in a tower.

Giraffes spend most of their day eating leaves. They eat acacia leaves.

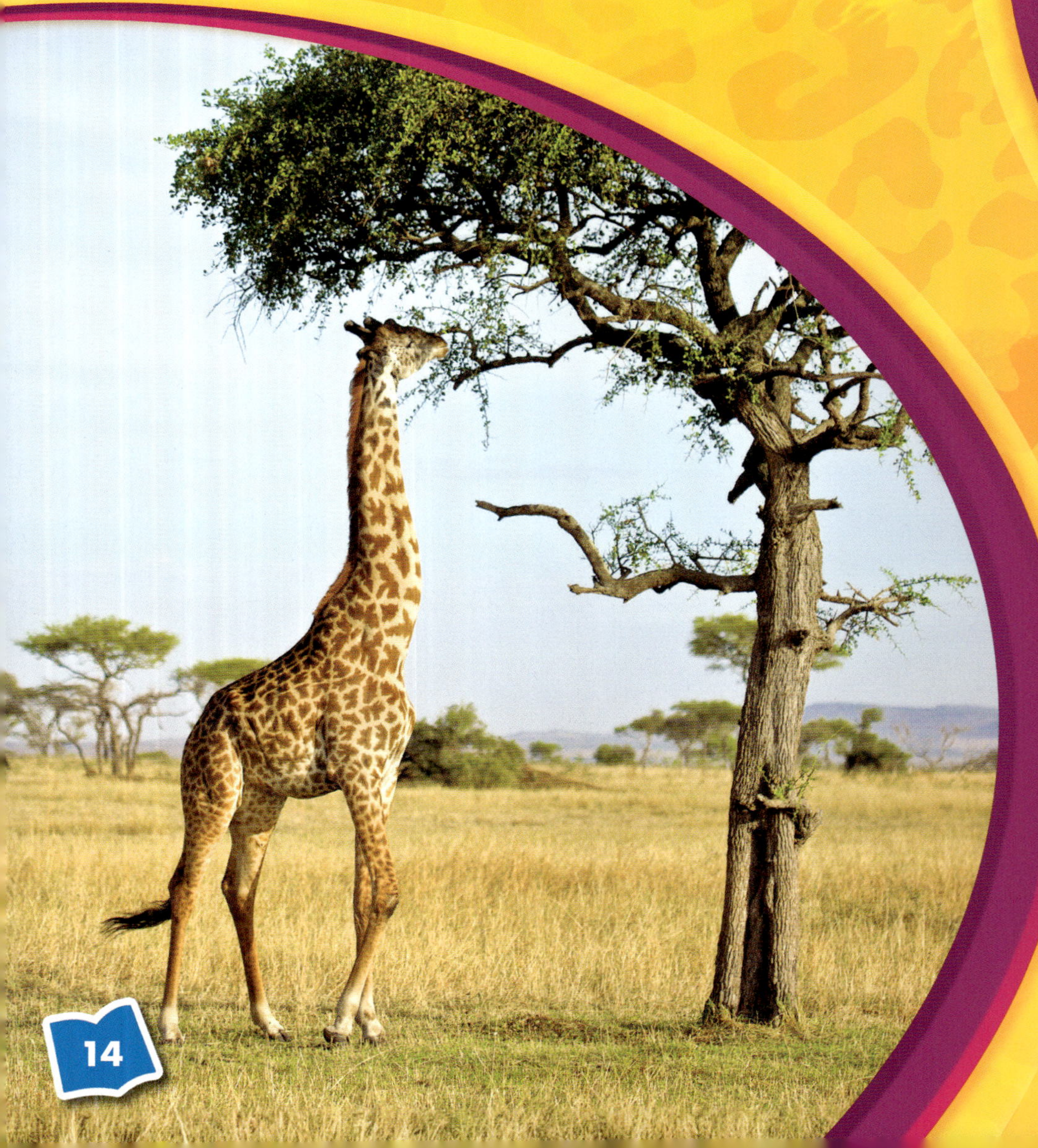

Their sticky **saliva** helps them swallow thorns.

Crocodiles, hyenas, and lions hunt giraffes. They attack when giraffes sleep and drink water.

Giraffe Food Web

Giraffes take short naps. They take turns watching for predators. This keeps towers safe!

Growing Up

Female giraffes give birth to one **calf** at a time. Calves can walk one hour after birth.

Soon, calves join a **nursery**. Mothers take turns watching them.

calf

Female giraffes often stay with their mothers. Males leave their mothers by age 2.

These tall animals can live for about 25 years!

Life of a Giraffe

Name of Babies

calves

Number of Babies

1

Time Spent with Mom

around 2 or more years

Life Span

about 25 years

Glossary

calf—baby giraffe

coats—the hair or fur covering some animals

mammals—warm-blooded animals that have backbones and feed their young milk

nursery—a group of young giraffes that are raised together

ossicones—short horns on giraffes' heads covered by skin and hair

pattern—the set of markings on an animal's fur

predators—animals that hunt other animals for food

saliva—a watery fluid in the mouth that breaks down food

savannas—flat grasslands with few trees

towers—groups of giraffes

To Learn More

AT THE LIBRARY

Barth, Kelley. *A Tower of Giraffes.* Parker, Colo.: The Child's World, 2024.

Brinker, Spencer. *Baby Giraffes.* Minneapolis, Minn.: Bearport Publishing Company, 2021.

Lynch, Seth. *A Tower of Giraffes.* New York, N.Y.: Gareth Stevens Publishing, 2022.

ON THE WEB

FACTSURFER

Factsurfer.com gives you a safe, fun way to find more information.

1. Go to www.factsurfer.com.
2. Enter "giraffes" into the search box and click 🔍.
3. Select your book cover to see a list of related content.

Index

Africa, 4
calf, 18, 19
coats, 6, 7
colors, 6
day, 14
females, 9, 18, 20
food, 14, 15, 17
forests, 12
legs, 10
life of a giraffe, 21
males, 8, 9, 20
mammals, 4
mothers, 18, 20
naps, 17
necks, 4
nursery, 18
ossicones, 10
pattern, 7
predators, 10, 16, 17
range, 4, 5
run, 10
saliva, 15
savannas, 12
size, 4, 8, 9, 10, 12, 21
spot a giraffe, 11
status, 5
towers, 13, 17
walk, 18
water, 16

The images in this book are reproduced through the courtesy of: Volodymyr Burdiak, front cover, front cover background, interior background; Design_Lands, front cover (giraffe icon); Trixy Gatto, p. 3; Jill Richardson King, p. 4; nwdph, p. 6; Samuel Avola Mungujakisa, p. 7; Kendal Swart, p. 8; duchy, p. 9; Independent birds, p. 10; Dmitry Pichugin, pp. 10-11; jaroslava V, p. 11; EcoPrint, p. 12; NSP-RF/ Alamy, p. 13; tonyzhao120, p. 14; marseus, p. 15; ArCaLu, pp. 16-17; Artush, p. 17 (crocodiles); Andrew M. Allport, p. 17 (hyenas); Manoj Kumar Tuteja, p. 17 (lions); Anita van den Broek, p. 17 (giraffe); dimas992, p. 17 (acacia leaves); Dr. Stefan Matthies, p. 18; Sergey Novikov, p. 19; Albert Beukhof, p. 20; Stacey Ann Alberts, p. 21; tomr, p. 21 (giraffe icon); FrentaN, p. 23.